SMOKESCREEN

POEMS

LONDYN RAYNE

THREE ⫶ OWLS
PUBLISHING

This is a work of fiction. Names, characters, places, and incidents are products of the author's imagination or are used fictitiously and are not to be construed as real. Any resemblance to actual events, locales, organizations, or persons, living or dead, is entirely coincidental.

This book may not be reproduced in whole or in part without written permission.

ISBN 978-1-7331920-9-5

www.threeowlspublishing.com

SMOKESCREEN. Copyright @ 2021 by Londyn Rayne. All rights reserved. Printed in the United States of America. Anyone may copy this work for non-commercial purposes.

*Dedicated to anyone who has ever suffered in silence
To their friends & family that didn't give up on them
And to Jesus, the only one who can truly rescue any of us*

TRACK LISTING

shadow	1
stranger	2
wilted : prologue	3
mercy	4
tonight	5
less broken	6
yellow	7
flowers	8
phantom	9
familiar	11
internalize	12
ravens	13
wilted : interlude : part 2	14
intricate	15
shift in shadows	16
staccato	18
wilted : interlude : part 3	19
concealed carry	21
lullaby	22
mirror	23
a sense of silence	24
wilted : interlude : part 4	26
broken record	27
recycled	28
tangible	29

shotgun	30
heroine	31
wilted : interlude : part 5	32
serpent	33
capture	35
trees	36
reminiscence	37
frostbite	39
pillar	40
hindsight	41
wilted : interlude : part 6	42
deceit	43
amputation	44
soundtrack	46
about midnight	47
graffiti	48
wilted : interlude : part 7	49
fractures	50
electric blue	51
phoenix	52
carpenter	53
key	55
wilted : epilogue	56
smokescreen	58
slain	59

And maybe
If you let me cry
I won't have to hide anymore

SHADOW

cast your fears upon your mind
left behind
by your darkness

light collapses
ashes ignite regret
to resurrect a side effect
perfect lies divide me

my shadow will be my death
come out, sun
and damage us

we die
despite the rumors
we are safe
with all the anger in us
we unite

my enemies defend me
give me peace

lost staring
at my overcast unknown

STRANGER

if you knew my thoughts
you wouldn't recognize me

WILTED - PROLOGUE

wilted and whimpering
dry and abandoned
thirsty and searching
for just a sip of mercy
but all i can see ends up being
a mirage

rain drops seem to skip me like rocks
why am i so easy to leave
unpicked
unable to speak
being unheard is identical
to being unseen

though my pain may be rooted in the past
it might be worth more
than what i would ask for it
the tag hangs a warning
of fragility and fatigue
while the receipt shows the origin
of the antique

i won't lie
but i will avoid the contagion
of apathetic critique
behavioral management
may never be adequate
pruning at the wrong time
won't assist the flower in the art of blooming
but i'll try again
i'll plant myself in a corner

a law unto herself
disciplined for becoming
a mourner;

MERCY

i believe my memories
were muted by a medley
of trauma and mercy

TONIGHT

my mind
is not kind tonight
i don't know if i can do this

my heart
is nervous tonight
it murmurs with pain
that fills the vacancy
where it's said to be beating
i gasp for breath
and grab my chest
as it aches and re-breaks
i'm sweating and trembling

my hope
is dying alone tonight
initial arrests are cardiac
the attacks are secondary
i react
laying flat
my only stability
is this hard floor like a splint
something that supports me
behind my back

my eyes
are burning tonight
after the fight to keep them open
in the straight lines of sustained wind
my sight has swollen shut
yet my tears still drain
pouring down the sides of my cheeks
flooding my ears
until i can't hear
you speak

LESS BROKEN

i'm comforted
when you cry with me
the mai tai of tears
is a remedy
to feel less
broken
let's be lonely
collectively
maybe our sharp creases
are actually
puzzle pieces
that fit in
each other's pictures

YELLOW

i will not lie down in this yellow casket
you picked out
even though
it shares the same color
as sunshine
it's a mascot of abandonment
i will not lay my head on this pillow of death
you picked out
even though
you say it's mine
this box of pine
will burn like sap
in the forest of my mind

FLOWERS

a daily stampede of flowers
with the scent of newspaper
i had a special little rose
the only part of home
that left with me
i hated when the others
got picked and separated
their bewildered faces looking back
is that how i looked?

PHANTOM

it's beyond what i scream
in the dark
your words cut through
and haunt my heart

numb because i have to be
i have to fight not to believe
that it was all ruined because of me

i try hard to ignore the evidence
that someone is always lying to me
through the mist
when the stories don't add up
i don't know who, but someone has to be

so i disguise my heart with a sheet
cut eyes in it so i can see
learn to despise what falls apart
play hide and seek with myself
trying to survive this
tug of war on my soul
i wish i could outrun the damage
but unlike you
it won't let me go

if you make me leave
please don't believe
that you'll ever see my ghost
i'll never get that close

i almost trusted you would listen
now i'm missing
with words unheard
you look right through me
like a distant apparition

if this isn't real like you want to think
why am i still waking up bleeding
never scarring
will i ever be okay?

i forget if i can forgive
if i can make it through this
i'll probably still be hurting

maybe you never thought i'd have to be brave
it taught me
you were afraid

FAMILIAR

i'm grieving people i haven't even lost yet
so when they leave
the sting will be
familiar

INTERNALIZE

the clock wants to chime
instead,
it can't tell time
it can't read the mind
or hold the hands
that won't rewind

the siren wants to warn
instead,
it mourns
the warpath
of the predicted storm

the church bell wants to ring
instead,
the celestial choir
in hell
begins to sing

you want to speak
instead,
silence manifests
as you can barely confess
you're weak

RAVENS

an unkindness
of words
this flock
forms a curse
that builds a nest
out of your bones
invading your rest
calling your soul
home

WILTED - INTERLUDE - PART 2

wilted and afraid
regretful and ashamed
unaware of habitual harassment
my petals are stained
some are absent
checkmate
covered in dirt
pretending i hate
is more acceptable
than admitting i hurt
concealing my care
is easier
than declaring how
the wounds hidden within me
have crafted an emotional execution
in the empty arena of my seclusion;

INTRICATE

how intricate
how colorful
are my bruises
blending together
attempting to camouflage abuses

my air is polluted
i choke as my voice is muted
when intimidation gets deadlier

my heart is heavier
than the fear
forcing itself on top of me

SHIFT IN SHADOWS

the infinite sky fills with light
eerie and peaceful
thickness saturates the air

as the moon rises
so does the tension

not a sliver is missing
from the dark rock
reflecting the sun

eyes glowing red
claws released
sharpened
like they've been craving
to run

the howling of my voice
as the wind blows
a shift in shadows

a dissimilar image appears
suddenly
mirrors deviate
and who you know
disappears

shrapnel remains
of the ghost of me
i thought a silver bullet slayed
these pieces appear when
being hunted by those who have pierced
a hole in my past

in their crosshairs they attach
their gaze
and track my movement as though
i'm still who they knew
but i know the truth
they're only able to see
stubborn traces and mimicry

of who i used to be

shapeshifting shadows dance
the moon finally exhausts the night
luminous spotlight now shines
on a tattered soul
who is terrified
of herself

STACCATO

dust and ash as thick as snow
an attic attacked by arson
flashes of burning embers
fall like staccato
disconnected

a flurry of infected flashbacks
forces my train of thought
to slip off the tracks

how do I rest this restless envy
of deathless souls that appear to be free

how much ice do i need
to tame these memories
swelling like flames

my spirit feels so empty
there's no portrait
merely a frame

WILTED - INTERLUDE - PART 3

wilted and tormented
my torrential tears aren't enough
to nourish the thirst within the petals
the layers of my heart
sunshine of the day won't fix it
it is not sufficient

my roots are planted in a shadow
the sun simply burns my bloodshot eyes
and aims a spotlight on the evidence
that i'm rotten
in the midst of what could be
a vibrant garden
i feel forgotten

potpourri may be
my only chance to be
separated from my roots that hold me
yes. they'll just burn me to make use
mixing my dry skin with spice
stirred in a bowl to soothe
they'll inhale the scent
of my remains
and recline in their careless domain

i wasn't suitable to grow
i know, i'm not presentable to show
a vase would reject me
lace would likely disrespect me

i could never be selected
to be put on display
i'd never be a gift that goes
from hand to hand
on a special day

they'd never want me to be seen
i'd never be cast for that scene
where the girl in love peels back
the layers of me
asking my petals to answer her hopeful question:

"does he love me?"

however
i can't help but notice
the dirt that splashes on me
is the same as all the others
so why am i so embarrassed
of my distressed colors?;

CONCEALED CARRY

some wear their hearts on their sleeve
and hide their scars underneath

LULLABY

twilight spirits revive my silent slumber
the alarm lights up my skeleton in dust and clouds
laying down beside neon moonlight
shadows fill the ceiling
where my nightmares go to dream

sever the sunset
as lightning tears fall
whispers howl, wind screams
prayers breathe upon my scars
keeping me afloat
following the sea

the mist cuts in
i run aground
the lies exist
i hear them growl

a legend lullaby in darkness
awakened by pastel starlight

follow those neon shadows
fall behind me, slow
listen to my song
go safely
back to sleep

MIRROR

sometimes i stare
at you
with my hollow eyes
because i'm dying
for you
to unravel my mind

A SENSE OF SILENCE

a cry for help
that went unnoticed
not because they missed it
they just didn't care

a song written but never heard
they played it as loud as they were allowed to
but musicians themselves are muted
if no one listens to their music

your secret getting tossed by the wind
of someone else's breath
what a deafening whisper

saying nothing
tends to insure the message is sent
sometimes silence is the loudest
my voice will ever get

grudges held like a hand you hold
for protection
lead to lives that end in regret

a friend's shoulder you used to cry on
is now so cold your tears would freeze

absent love that leaves you
steeped in insecurity
sipping on lies that shimmer
comfort and shine
with chemicals—
the steam ascends with an aroma
that verifies
the additives are artificial

instant burn blisters on your tongue
with the aftertaste of bitter words
liquor stings
before it washes you numb

a smile can blanket a bed of pain
a banquet can disguise a bloodline
flooded with people shifting blame
feasting on scraps
choking on pride
spitting out names

it's too hard
just throw my heart in a junk drawer
let it get lost
i'll dig for it later when someone needs it
to open a door

WILTED - INTERLUDE - PART 4

wilted and confused
now intimate with abuse
i fell charmed
with the false yet friendly feeling of darkness

it became comfortable
almost serene
a leaf floating gently down the stream
alone with my thoughts
wishing daydreams would intervene

but i'm starting to see
a subtle enlivening
like that of a homecoming
a cheer for the winning team
my jersey that reads "Misery"
is no longer an option
despair has revealed itself
as a prison cell for orphans
and i seek adoption

i can't take cover in the familiar shade
i was planted in
like a recluse that got caught
entangled in a web
she didn't spin

again and again
i need to lean in
to the light
i understand now
i require a specific type to live
to thaw out my bitterness

enduring the clock
or hoping it would stop
i don't see a difference
the whole time i've been ticking
behind my lock;

BROKEN RECORD

i don't want a record
of being broken

RECYCLED

paranoid
i started to believe the hype
that i
was trash
easy
to throw out

mocked
for where i slept
sleep was illusive
i mostly wept
as i was learning so fast
how to regret

there was nowhere to hide
i would always seek but never find
count to ten
ready or not
i drifted into a polluted mind
i lied to myself
at least i tried

hostile confusion
reputation in ruins
truth didn't stand a chance

anxiety found my hiding place
and consumed me completely
effectively masking the real me
suffocated
i had become
everything i hated

TANGIBLE

you're the cliche
sand slipping away
but then sometimes, it rains
your texture
will change
and, until you evaporate
i'm able to hold you

SHOTGUN

inhale the overcast
that numbs my past
this is not me

adore the hands
that keep the shots poured
smile as i fall blissfully to the floor
this is not me

synthetic rest
cleansing my thoughts
at least momentarily
exhale my worries
they flee in a haze of dissipating fog
this is not me

a strobe light
inducing a trance
a beat
introducing a dance
taking advantage
escapism clings
this is not me

HEROINE

i did not stand
point blank
i did not make
myself a target
for your bullets
voluntarily

so my exit wounds
don't make me a hero

WILTED - INTERLUDE - PART 5

wilted and molting
my heart's layers
are peeling like petals
on a neglected rose
baptized in rejected tears
that fall like snowflakes

slight warmth is thawing
my memories
the trauma froze
still cold
but softening

petals, one by one
gracefully descend
to meet the others
disassembling
until all that's left
is a bare stem
full of thorns
each as sharp as the words
that pierced my soul;

SERPENT

on the eve of betrayal
how did you sleep?

CAPTURE

i can't bring myself to burn it
i'd rather preserve the memory
than hoard an empty frame

TREES

the trees are letting go
as am i
the leaves that fall
are still lovely
laying on rock bottom
arguably at their height
of beauty
rich in warm hues
ironic that so many
love the artistry
in a season
of abundant death

the leaves must fall
they have to be released from the limbs
that once held them for so long
they have to make room
for something green
something new
to bloom

REMINISCENCE

the crackling campfire sings a hymn
ghost stories and vampire stings
accompanied by a brisk breeze
candles lit
with the spice of burning leaves
a few days before halloween
orange, yellow, and brown
jewelry on trees

driving at night
nestled within the winding country roads
alone
with the windows down
heat on and music higher
the speed makes the warm wind
a calming sound

i watch nature flutter in the streetlights
landing in a bed of damp roads
still shining from the evening downpour

clothed with cutoff shorts
comforted by a hoodie for warmth
chilled from my skin
soaked in sunburn
as my chlorine stained hair hits the pillow
i still hear the water splash
falling asleep quick with
chemical eyes too heavy to lift

ecstatic lightning and rolling thunder
the perfume in the air signals rain
ambient weather on a melancholy day

colors that can't be replicated by ink or paint
projected on the sky
a coral horizon
violet shadows behind the mosaic of clouds
provide vivid contrast
while suspended in the vast sapphire

a city skyline after dark
lights in symmetry with the stars
how wispy clouds see themselves
in a sea of glass

freshly cut grass
and spilled gasoline
leather jackets and ripped jeans
hypnotizing glitter
accessorized with dirt
the scent of stale hops
spilled on my shirt

the concert
when the bassline becomes my throbbing heartbeat
hearing that song live
the one i didn't even write
that perfectly tells my story

when someone i miss
seems excited to see me
when someone i trust
also trusts me

when anyone randomly tells me
they love me
when you realize
that person wants to kiss you too
the anticipation
a few seconds before you do

a hug i can hang on to
the kind of embrace that stays
and takes a while
to fade away

contagious laughter that keeps going
infectious tears that result in growing
closer

inside jokes with those who know
the kind you can sometimes tell
with just a look
and in that moment
you relive a memory
together

old pictures with friends
that are no longer your friends
the smile mixed with tears
remembering how it was before

simplicity
that intricately
connects memories
for all of us
as we reminisce

FROSTBITE

i believe it's okay to feel
and feel strongly
numbness only seems appealing
because it's so much easier

though ice may shine like glass
masquerading as strength
its character is cold— flat and faceless

don't let bitterness
bite you with its poisonous fangs
crafted in apathy
releasing a sting
shaming you
for retaining warmth

PILLAR

somehow
your beautiful ruins
still stand strong enough
to hold me up

HINDSIGHT

for every night
i clawed through by myself
when i didn't know how
to ask for help

for every shower
that the water drowned out
the sound of my crying
afraid of being called a coward
so i cowered
as my tears disappeared down the drain
uncomforted

for every time i tried
desperately
to be the best version of happy
i knew how to be
while simultaneously hosting
a gnawing tension inside of me

for every time i chose
to stay quiet
knowing i would replay the show
in silence
it would tread back and forth
in my head
i should have just said something
so the "what ifs" wouldn't be on repeat

i never wanted to be alone
but i knew i needed privacy
so i could hurt as bad i needed to
without the risk of hurting someone else too

for every time i said
i fought alone
i found out it was fear
lying to me
i was never alone
i was scared
but you were here

WILTED - INTERLUDE - PART 6

wilted and kneeling
i see clearly
how i spent so much time feeling
overwhelmed
striving to pick up fallen petals
prying them off the ground
desperately trying to rehydrate them
with no irrigation system

coping
only by sticking them back together
with faux strength
coloring them red
with leftover paint

some days
i may have passed
as a living rose
but it would never last
i'd start itching from the dryness
a rash
that resembled shyness

unmasked
spackle hid my puncture wounds
tucked inside the paneling of my soul and mind
and as petals continued to collapse
a near trigger
a brief fear of relapse
as i watched petals i was so attached to
fade to black;

DECEIT

hypocrisy
spoken beautifully
sounds like honesty

AMPUTATION

the serpent of bondage
constricting my heart
weighing down my chest
my lungs can't expand wide enough
to catch my breath

leather whips
excavating my skin
one lies around my neck
if sudden moves are detected
it starts closing in

spikes in my mouth
piercing my lips
snatching my tongue
my words slip

chains so tightly bound
they slice my wrists
holding my hands down
so anything i could touch
that might turn to gold
is off limits

my legs locked
unable to walk
every step i would take-
if i were able
would carry me further away
from my own mistakes

i can't break away from myself
in despair i try to escape
and then you...

you came into my chamber
you showed me
slowly
how you were removing
the torture devices clinging to me
you explained

how they were embossed so severely
that prying them away would be painful
and uneasy
but if i were willing
to surrender to your rescue
i'd realize that you
were already doing it for me
and the freedom
was the unfamiliar hope
i was feeling

you told me
i'd learn a new language
when you untangled my vocal cords
you cut away the gag and ropes
with your divine sword

you warned me
that after being tied up for so long
it would take time
to stand up straight
i'd be stiff for awhile
but you promised sufficient grace

you assured me
that things would not remain blurry
for much longer

you displayed
your distinct and delicate power
you let me feel
your undeniable bedside manner
as you tended to my gaping wounds
that were left after amputating
all that had become attached to me
that wasn't part of you

SOUNDTRACK

the soundtrack to my fantasy
you are the visual
if heaven is ecstasy
home is fictional
if death is freedom
breath is captivity

ABOUT MIDNIGHT

like when blood rushes back vigorously
to a place in your mind that had fallen asleep

i felt that tender, yet refreshing flow
of healing race into my soul
as i confessed
and tried to keep from crying
out too loud
i was able to let go
of everything
i could never control
about midnight
on the eve of redemption
even in darkness
light pours power into pain

GRAFFITI

some don't cut to kill
some cut to feel
something different
than what's already killing them
bruising hides the hurt the heart can't hold

i knew this was panic putting up a fight
just as i know the sun dies at night

my face would go numb
stiff with tension
my eyes fell dim with repetition

i'd rather battle a fever that breaks the skin
than fail to heal my severed heart again

anguish disguised by anger
i would self insert
and send an alert that was hard to recognize
praying that secretly someone would reach to me
and love me through the dense lies
that preached to me

our own blood will never wash the sorrow away
it's simply a reminder
a dramatic display
that we're still alive

when graffiti scrawls the exterior walls
of the temple
you always know what's really inside
only you can see the interior design
which is why
you're so gentle

you know how to find us
with an empathetic embrace
only you can erase
the trademarks of shame
and replace them with birthmarks
sealed with your name

WILTED - INTERLUDE - PART 7

wilted and healing
i was left skinned and peeling
shedding— simulated blooming
now unable to be recognized
as a rose

i didn't have the capability
to live in conditions so frigid and cold

to find truth
it took stripping away
all of my protective petals
that served as an army with shields
as they lowered their screens
it allowed the gardener
to mend
and settle my soul

somehow
he still saw beauty
in his wilted rose

FRACTURES

the fractures
of my broken heart
have allowed an unfailing love
to flow in

ELECTRIC BLUE

dusk
panoramic view
ominous clouds
eclipsing
the electric blue
striking lightning
reflecting you

the sky was on fire
trembling
like thunder
a disciple
of the electronic choir

neon army
glowing in peace
stillness surrounded
by chaos and electricity

city lights captured
in slow shutter speed
every hair raised
electrocuted with praise

since the creation
of time
creator divine
i
in seeking
am without excuse

PHOENIX

dry soul like an ashtray
trash that smolders
a charcoal heart
of decay
performance of flames
the flesh burns away
in a stunning array
a flash of renewal
spirit ablaze

CARPENTER

the carpenter
became the beautiful
intricate detail
the finishing touch
in the woodwork

the carpenter
climbed the tree
dead load momentarily
live load eternally

dovetail strength
rested upon you
the force that resisted
your body from splintering
while disfigured
tortured and shivering
under blood drenched lumber

carpenter
why did you suffer for me?
passion
woke you from your slumber
miracle
sign
wonder

your name is my king
you transferred me
out of darkness
into royalty
crucify my flesh
as i seek your throne
resurrect my life with yours
as i die to my own

pierce
through my spirit
fill me with yours
fierce
in appearance

suit me for war

the knives in my back
void
by the nails through your hands
my blood transfused
by the blood of the lamb

the cuts on my limbs
eliminated
by the limbs that beat you
unrecognizable

you reversed my grave
as you inhaled your first
breath
of musty tomb air
embarrassing death
my broken heart
healed
by your body broken for me

i'll wear my scars
like you wear yours
adorned in a wardrobe
of victory

KEY

the heat is softer
it's easier to inhale the cleaner air
crossing over the barrier
leaving a city of toxicity
i wandered too long
with no visibility

through the pollution
i needed a key
freedom had to rescue me
from the illusion of safety

my eyes grew deadlocked
on your voice

then one day
i returned to the opening scene
this time
i had you with me

you turned the key
so i could see
the pain i swore to secrecy
was no longer a mystery
it let go of me
and i was finally able to release
the air i was gripping
voluntarily

end scene
this is my story
but it was never about me

WILTED - EPILOGUE

transplanted
exposed and swarmed by thorns
recounting every petal that fell
with each one
a story to tell someone else that
"he loves me"
never did he love me not

my soul is bought
my ground transformed
my thorns matured into sharpened swords
twisting together resembling a crown
like the one my king wore
when the enemy failed
at holding him down

my skeleton key
that unlocks every chain and opens every door
the veil was torn
he re-planted me
and watered me

my roots were dug up and reclaimed
validating my pain and showing me how
not a second of what i went through was in vain

so i thought they loved me not
but who are they to save me?
i'm redeemed, i'm free
and now with every petal to ever fall again
i'll always be reminded
that "he loves me"

the old has passed away
though the dried up pieces still have beauty
my life may fade, but it will never decay
as he resurrects all new petals
and stamps them with his name

i'm no longer wilted
i'm on eternal display
a rose held by a king
yet just a small piece
of a heavenly arrangement
a holy bouquet

he once prayed in his own garden
on the eve of being betrayed
and wept
with precious crimson grace
love dripping down
and sweat pouring from his face

he hung on a tree
as his crown sat crooked on his head
the crowd, not knowing
he'd sit perfectly on a throne
in just a few days
they watched as puddles of sovereign blood
evaporated

they mispronounced him as dead
then he arose
and now that same crimson grace
fell down on me like rain
repainting
a once wilted
now regal rose
red

SMOKESCREEN

title track
may my faith never act
as a smokescreen
empty flattery
concealing authenticity

flames are ascending
receiving deliverance
from their beloved counterfeit cathedrals
standing staunch underneath
a twisted steeple
this deception
is lethal

hidden from the enemy
yet a target of his scrutiny
i observed so much as i suffered distantly

i believe we can be healed instantly
i believe healing is an odyssey
i believe i am already healed

SLAIN

i'm a black sheep
following the slain lamb

www.ingramcontent.com/pod-product-compliance
Lightning Source LLC
Chambersburg PA
CBHW011131070526
44583CB00023B/2993